D0857785

creatures of the sea

Sea Turtles

Kris Hirschmann

KIDHAVEN PRESS

An imprint of Thomson Gale, a part of The Thomson Corporation

THOMSON

GALE

Detroit • New York • San Francisco • San Diego • New Haven, Conn.
Waterville, Maine • London • Munich

© 2005 Thomson Gale, a part of The Thomson Corporation.

Thomson and Star Logo are trademarks and Gale and KidHaven Press are registered trademarks used herein under license.

For more information, contact
KidHaven Press
27500 Drake Rd.
Farmington Hills, MI 48331-3535
Or you can visit our Internet site at http://www.gale.com

Picture Credits:
Cover photo: © Stuart Westmorland/CORBIS. Inside: © AP/ The Daily News, 41; © Anthony Banister; Galo Images/CORBIS, 36; © Jonathon Blair/CORBIS, 32; © Tim Davis/CORBIS, 9; © DiMaggio/Kalish/COR-BIS, 37; © Owen Franken/CORBIS, 39; © Ivan Fulcher/CORBIS, 33; Joseph Giddings, 10-11,12-13,15, 42–43; © Roger De La Harpe; Gallo Images/CORBIS, 6; © National Geographic/Getty Images, 29; © Reuters/Landov, 16; © Reuters/Made Sudane/Landov, 5; © Linda Richardson/CORBIS, 21, 25; © Jeffrey L. Rottman/CORBIS, 20, 31, 40; © Kevin Schafer/CORBIS, 23; © Sea World of California/CORBIS, 28; © SUKREE SUKPLANG/Reuters/CORBIS, 7; © Juan Carlos Ulate/Reuters/CORBIS, 17, 22.

LIBRARY OF CONGRESS CATALOGING-IN-PUBLICATION DATA

Hirschmann, Kris, 1967–
    Sea turtles / by Kris Hirschmann.
        p. cm. — (Creatures of the sea)
    Includes bibliographical references and index.
    Contents: Sea turtle bodies and basics—A long life—The search for food—Sea turtles in danger.
    ISBN 0-7377-3011-0 (hard cover : alk. paper)
    1. Sea turtles—Juvenile literature. I. Title.
    QL666.C536H56 2005
    597.92'8—dc22
                                                                        2004027040

Printed in the United States of America

Table of Contents

Tracking Sea Turtles

M ost ocean creatures spend their entire lives underwater. But sea turtles do not. Female sea turtles lay their eggs on land, so they regularly leave the ocean during nesting season. This habit brings sea turtles into frequent contact with humans, making them one of the sea's best-known and best-loved creatures.

Because they are so easy to find and watch, nesting sea turtles have been described countless times by scientists. Much less is known, however, about the underwater life of the sea turtle. After laying eggs, these animals return to the sea and swim away. They become hard to find for study. Researchers wearing scuba gear have learned about sea turtles by watching them for a few moments at a time. But questions about turtles still remain. Scientists want to learn where sea turtles live as babies, what territories turtles roam, and what migration routes turtles follow. For most kinds of sea turtles, these questions have not been answered.

A young tourist smiles as she returns a captive green sea turtle to the ocean in Bali, Indonesia.

To uncover this information and more, modern scientists use several methods to track wild sea turtles. The simplest method is clipping a numbered metal tag to a turtle's flipper. Using this tag, scientists can identify a sea turtle no matter where it shows up. Scientists also attach satellite tracking devices to turtles' shells. Every time a tagged sea turtle approaches the water's surface, the device sends information about the turtle's location to satellites high in the sky. The satellites then transmit the information to scientists' computers. Some scientists even take blood from sea turtles and use it to

A scientist from South Africa tags a baby loggerhead turtle as part of a research project.

Marine biologists from Thailand attach a satellite-tracking antenna to the back of a 30-year-old male green sea turtle that was swept inland during the 2004 tsunami.

run genetic tests. This kind of tracking can identify related sea turtle populations around the world.

Tracking sea turtles may help scientists to learn more about the daily lives of these magnificent creatures. This knowledge may, in turn, help people to come up with new ways of protecting sea turtles, which are in danger of extinction.

Sea Turtle Bodies and Basics

Land turtles are known for being slow moving and clumsy. But sea turtles are different. Supported by water, even the largest sea turtle is not bothered by its weight. It swims quickly and gracefully from place to place, easy and comfortable in its ocean home.

All sea turtles belong to the scientific suborder **Cryptodira**, which also includes freshwater turtles, snapping turtles, tortoises, and soft-shelled turtles. The word *Cryptodira* comes from Greek words meaning "hidden-necked." The suborder got this name because some turtles can pull their necks and heads into their shells. While sea turtles cannot do this, they are still included in this scientific group.

Sea turtles and their relatives are reptiles. Like all reptiles, they are cold blooded, which means they do not maintain a consistent body temperature. Instead, their temperature goes up and down depending on the outside environment.

Finding Sea Turtles

Because sea turtles cannot control their body temperature, they must stay in warm waters to keep from

Sea turtles are expert swimmers. Here, a green sea turtle swims gracefully above the ocean floor.

getting too cold. For this reason, sea turtles are most common in the tropical waters near the earth's equator. They may also live in temperate (cool but not cold) waters. The only type of sea turtle that wanders outside this range is the leatherback. It is sometimes seen as far north as Canada, where water temperatures reach only 40 degrees Fahrenheit (4.5 degrees Celsius).

Sea turtles can be found all over the world in waters within their comfortable temperature range. These creatures live in all types of saltwater bodies, including oceans, seas, lagoons, and bays. They may also

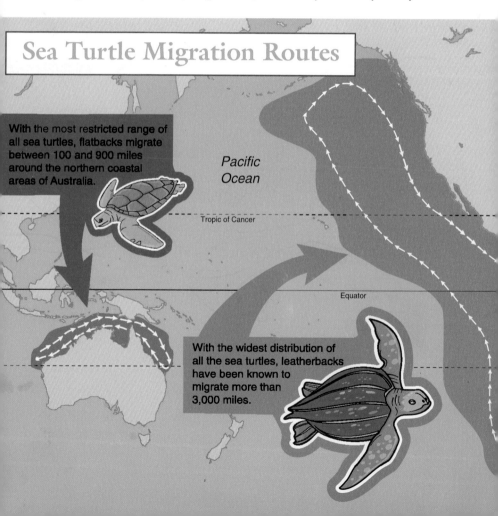

Sea Turtle Migration Routes

With the most restricted range of all sea turtles, flatbacks migrate between 100 and 900 miles around the northern coastal areas of Australia.

Pacific Ocean

Tropic of Cancer

Equator

With the widest distribution of all the sea turtles, leatherbacks have been known to migrate more than 3,000 miles.

swim into the partly salty water at the mouths of rivers. Most sea turtles live near land, but some spend time in the open sea.

Some populations of sea turtles stick to one small home range throughout their lives. Most sea turtles, however, are migrators. It is very common for sea turtles to travel several hundred miles (500km or more) between their nesting and feeding grounds each year. Some groups travel even farther, swimming more than 3,000 miles (4,827km) each way between their summer and winter homes.

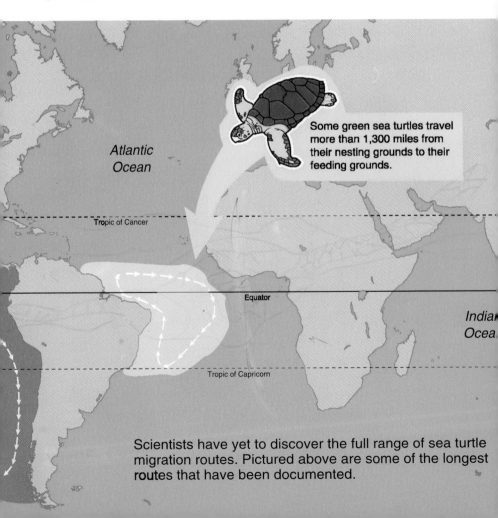

Atlantic
Ocean

Some green sea turtles travel more than 1,300 miles from their nesting grounds to their feeding grounds.

Tropic of Cancer

Equator

Indian
Ocean

Tropic of Capricorn

Scientists have yet to discover the full range of sea turtle migration routes. Pictured above are some of the longest routes that have been documented.

Types of Sea Turtles

There are eight species of sea turtles: the loggerhead, the hawksbill, the flatback, the Kemp's ridley, the olive ridley, the leatherback, the green sea turtle, and the black sea turtle. Some scientists think green and black sea turtles are members of the same species because they are very similar at a genetic level. But because these creatures have some striking differences in color and shape, most scientists agree that they should be considered separate species.

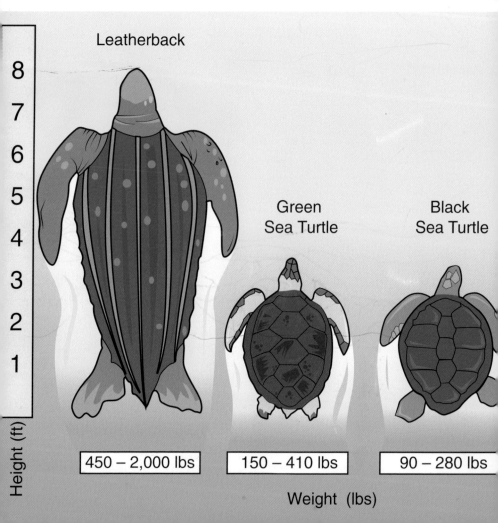

Leatherback

Green Sea Turtle

Black Sea Turtle

450 – 2,000 lbs

150 – 410 lbs

90 – 280 lbs

Height (ft)

8
7
6
5
4
3
2
1

Weight (lbs)

There is a wide range of sizes within the sea turtle family. On average, the smallest species are the Kemp's ridley and olive ridley, which may measure as little as 22 inches (51cm) from end to end and weigh just 66 pounds (30kg). The largest species is the leatherback, which can grow to 6 feet (1.8m) in length and may weigh more than 1,000 pounds (454kg). Occasionally leatherbacks get even bigger than this. Fishermen once captured an enormous one measuring 8.4 feet (2.6m) from tip to tip and weighing more than 2,000 pounds (907kg).

Comparing Sea Turtles

Loggerhead

Flatback

Hawksbill

Kemp's and Olive Ridley

145 – 225 lbs   130 – 185 lbs   60 – 190 lbs   65 – 110 lbs

Size is not the only difference among sea turtle species. The colors of different sea turtles also vary. The ridleys and the flatback, for example, are green-gray. Loggerheads are reddish brown, and leatherbacks are brown or black. The hawksbill turtle has an especially beautiful brown-and-cream shell. The shell of this animal is the source of a material called tortoise-shell, which is sometimes made into eyeglass frames, combs, and other objects.

The green sea turtle is not green, as its name suggests. It is usually brown, black, or gray, with darker streaks and spots. This animal gets its name from a thick layer of green fat within its body.

An Armored Body

The sea turtle's best-known feature is its thick shell. The upper part, or back, of the turtle's shell is called the **carapace**. In all species except the leatherback, the underside of the carapace is made from the turtle's flattened ribs, and the turtle's spine is connected to the bottom of the carapace. The lower part, or belly, of the shell is called the **plastron**. Gaps at the front and the back of the shell allow the turtle's head, flipper-like legs, and tail to stick out.

In most sea turtles, the carapace is covered by tough scales called **scutes**. The scutes are made of **keratin**, the same material that makes human hair and fingernails. Scutes are hard enough to protect the sea turtle's soft body, but flexible enough to bend under pressure. Only one species of sea turtle, the leatherback, does not have scutes. Instead, these animals' backs are covered by thick leather. Raised rows of cartilage beneath the leather give the shell a ribbed look.

The leatherback's ridged shell makes this turtle especially easy to identify. But other sea turtles can also be identified by the shape of their carapace. The carapace of the hawksbill turtle, for example, is jagged along the rear edge. Olive ridleys have heart-shaped

Anatomy of the Sea Turtle

Sea turtles have excellent underwater vision.

Their powerful back flippers and tail help sea turtles steer through the water.

For ease of breathing out of the water, sea turtles' nostrils are on top of their snout.

Carapace (upper outer shell)

Eardrums and bones inside the sea turtle's head pick up sound vibrations.

Plastron (lower outer shell)

Sea turtles use their strong front legs for swimming.

carapaces, and the carapaces of flatbacks are flat and turn up along the edges. Different numbers and arrangements of scutes on the shell also help scientists to identify sea turtle species.

A group of volunteers on a beach in Indonesia releases an enormous leatherback turtle into the wild.

Like all sea turtles, this ridley turtle must poke its nose above the water's surface to breathe.

Breathing Air

Whatever they look like, all sea turtles breathe air, not water. To make breathing easy, the sea turtle's nostrils are found on top of its snout. A sea turtle needs to poke just the tip of its nose out of the water to suck in a fresh lungful of oxygen. Meanwhile, the rest of the body remains safely hidden beneath the water's surface.

Most of the time, sea turtles stay underwater just a few minutes before coming to the surface for a quick breath. However, these creatures can go much longer without breathing if they want to. Green sea turtles in particular are known for spending lots of time underwater. These animals often take naps on the sea floor and can hold their breath for up to five hours. But this is nothing compared to black sea turtles, which **hibernate** underwater during the chilliest parts of the year. When winter arrives, these creatures bury themselves in the cold mud of the Gulf of California and go to sleep for several months at a time.

When staying underwater for long periods, a sea turtle slows its heart rate dramatically to save oxygen. A resting sea turtle's heart may beat as little as once every nine minutes. Anything that raises the heart rate—strong swimming, for example, or quick, panicky movement—uses up oxygen and makes it necessary for a sea turtle to breathe more often. If the turtle cannot reach air when it needs to breathe, it will drown. Luckily for sea turtles, there are very few things in the ocean that block the way to the sea surface. So it is not usually a problem for these creatures to swim to the surface whenever they want to. Under normal circumstances, sea turtles are well equipped to get all the air—and everything else—they need to survive.

chapter 2

A Long Life

S ea turtles are long-lived creatures. A healthy indi-
vidual can live up to one hundred years in the wild.
During most of this life span, a sea turtle keeps to itself. But at certain times of the year, sea turtles come
together briefly to mate and create new sea turtles.

Mating

For most sea turtles, springtime is mating season. At
this time of the year, females release chemicals into the
water to signal that they are ready to mate. Males smell
the chemicals and approach the females. Sometimes
several males come after the same female. When this
happens, the males fight with each other, pushing and
biting as they try to get closer to the female sea turtle.

Eventually one male wins the battle. He climbs
onto the female's back and presses his plastron against
his mate's carapace. He also uses long claws on his front
and rear flippers to grasp the edges of the female's shell.

These mating green sea turtles may remain locked together for hours until the female's body is full of fertilized eggs.

The male is not gentle when he does this. A male sea turtle sometimes grabs so hard that he gouges the female's shell and tears the skin on her shoulders. He does this partly to make sure his mate does not escape. He is also trying to keep himself from being torn loose by other male sea turtles, which may continue to attack throughout the mating process.

Once the male has a good grip, the pair is ready to mate. The male's sex organs are located inside his long tail. The male sea turtle puts this tail under the back edge of the female's shell and begins to pass sperm into the female's body. This process can last for hours. The two sea turtles remain locked together until the mating is complete.

When the mating process is over, the male and female sea turtles break apart and go their separate ways. Her body full of fertilized eggs, the female swims toward the same beach where she herself was hatched.

Laying Eggs

The egg-laden female approaches the beach, usually at night. She floats just offshore for a little while, looking and listening for danger. If she senses none, she swims to the water's edge and begins crawling up the beach. Before long the female reaches the soft, dry sand on the upper part of the beach. Once there, she uses her front flippers to dig a pit for her body. She settles herself into the pit and starts digging again, this time with her rear flippers. She continues digging until the hole is as wide and as deep as she can make it.

When the digging is done, the female positions her body over the hole and starts laying leathery eggs that look like ping-pong balls. The eggs leave her body in a gooey stream of mucus. Depending on the species, the sea turtle will lay

A loggerhead turtle lays her soft, slippery eggs in a hole she has dug on the beach to protect them.

anywhere from 50 to 200 eggs, with the average being between 80 and 120. The eggs pile up in a soft, slippery mass as they drop into the hole.

When all of the eggs have been laid, the sea turtle uses her rear flippers to push sand back into the hole. She packs the sand down with her body and uses her front flippers to rake the sand over the nest, hiding it from predators. Then the tired sea turtle drags herself back to the water's edge, slips into the sea, and swims away. Her egg-laying duties are done—but not for long. Mating season is just beginning, and a female sea turtle will repeat the breeding and nesting process up to nine times during a single cycle.

A large group of olive ridley sea turtles nests together on a beach in Costa Rica.

A tiny green sea turtle breaks out of its shell on a beach on Ascension Island in the Atlantic Ocean.

Most sea turtles nest alone. Kemp's ridleys and olive ridleys, however, nest in gatherings called **arribadas**. The largest arribada ever seen by humans occurred in 1947, when about forty thousand female Kemp's ridleys came ashore on a remote beach in Mexico.

The Eggs Hatch

Once they are laid, the eggs start to develop. The amount of time it takes for the eggs to mature depends on the sand's temperature. If the sand is warm, development may take as little as forty-five days. If it is cool, the eggs may take seventy days to hatch. Temperature also affects the sex of the **embryos** inside the eggs. If the average temperature is high, the nest will produce mostly females. If the average temperature is low, the nest will produce mostly males. Temperatures in the middle produce a mix of sexes.

When the embryos are fully developed, they break out of their shells. The newly hatched sea turtles are only about 1 to 2 inches (2.5 to 5cm) long, and they look like miniature adults. As a group, the little creatures begin digging upward. It takes the nest several days to reach the surface. Once there, the baby sea turtles rest beneath a thin layer of sand and wait for night to fall. As soon as it does, the turtles burst out of their nest in a wiggling, flipper-waving group. They look for the brightest part of their new world—on darkened beaches, usually the moon reflecting off the ocean—and head toward the light.

Before long the newly hatched turtles reach the water's edge, where they are swept out to sea. The creatures flap their little flippers frantically, pushing themselves farther and farther away from their hatching grounds. The young sea turtles continue flapping in a **swimming frenzy** that lasts twenty-four to forty-eight hours. At the end of this time, the new sea turtles finally start to relax. They are far from the beach and all the dangers it holds, and they are ready to start their lives in the ocean.

Growing Up

At this point most young sea turtles become hard to find. In fact, the early part of the sea turtle's life is called the **lost year** because so little is known about this period. Scientists think young sea turtles probably live far out at sea, riding the ocean currents and hiding in patches of seaweed or other debris. During

Two loggerhead hatchlings off the Florida coast beat their flippers frantically as they make their way out to sea.

this time, the sea turtles grow quickly. A green sea turtle, for example, can add nearly a pound (0.45kg) in weight and half an inch (1.3cm) in length each month during its first year.

By the time it is a few years old, a sea turtle is much larger and stronger than it was when it hatched. The turtle heads back toward land and takes up life along a comfortable coastline. Its growth rate slows down, but does not stop. The sea turtle will continue to get bigger and bigger as long as it lives.

Depending on the species, sea turtles reach maturity somewhere between three and fifty years of age. This means they are ready to mate. Male sea turtles will mate every year for the rest of their lives, while females will mate and nest every two or three years. Scientists estimate that most sea turtles have about thirty years during which they can reproduce. This means that a female can lay thousands of eggs during her life. With luck, some of the young turtles that hatch from these eggs will survive, continuing the sea turtle cycle of life.

3

The Search
for Food

S ea turtles are big, active creatures. Because of this, they must eat plenty of food to give them the energy they need to survive. So sea turtles spend lots of time looking for their next meal.

What Sea Turtles Eat

Sea turtles of different species have very different diets. Loggerheads and ridleys, for example, eat mostly hard food. These species feast on crabs, mollusks, shrimp, and other tough-shelled creatures. For this reason, loggerheads and ridleys have strong beaks that are good for crushing and grinding.

Leatherbacks, on the other hand, do not like hard food. These sea turtles eat only jellyfish and other soft foods. The leatherback's jaws are so delicate, in fact,

This loggerhead turtle's strong beak helps it crush and grind the tough shells of crabs, mollusks, and other hard-shelled creatures.

that they would be damaged by chewing on anything hard. To help the leatherback hold on to its food, its mouth and throat are lined with spines that spear prey as it eats. This prevents slippery morsels from sliding out of the leatherback's mouth.

During the earliest part of their lives, green and black sea turtles eat both hard and soft foods of all types. These animals enjoy jellyfish, crustaceans, and many other small creatures. After the lost year, however, green and black sea turtles move toward the shore and start eating plants rather than animals. They eat mostly algae and sea grasses for the rest of their lives.

Hawksbills have the most unusual diet of any sea turtle species. These animals eat mostly sponges. Most sea creatures will not bite sponges because their bodies are full of tiny sharp spikes. But these spikes do not seem to bother the hawksbill. Even though they pierce the flesh of the hawksbill's intestines, they do not do the turtle any lasting harm.

Not much is known about the eating habits of flatbacks. Scientists believe that they will eat almost anything they can find, including both plants and animals.

A hawksbill sea turtle hunts for sponges along a coral reef near the Florida coast.

Where Sea Turtles Hunt

How and where a sea turtle hunts depends on the type of food it eats. Leatherbacks, which prefer jellyfish above all other meals, swim high and low in search of food. At night, when jellyfish mass in shallow regions, leatherbacks make short hunting dives. But during the daytime, when jellyfish move deeper into the water, leatherbacks must dive far below the sea surface to capture their prey. Scientists tracking one leatherback recorded a hunting dive of 3,900 feet (1,189m). No other species of sea turtle travels this deep into the ocean.

Although they do not dive as deep as leatherbacks, loggerheads and ridleys also dive in search of food. These turtles swim down to the sea floor to look for shrimp, crabs, snails, and all the other bottom-dwelling creatures they like to eat. They may go as deep as 500 feet (152m) to find the food they need to survive.

Other species of sea turtles tend to be shallow-water hunters. Green and black sea turtles in particular stick to shallow regions, since deep water is too dark to support the plant life they eat. Flatbacks also seem to prefer the shallow waters near shore. And hawksbills, with their sponge diet, forage on coral reefs. These animals are even shaped to suit their hunting habits. The hawksbill's head is long and narrow—perfect for sticking into holes and cracks in the reef.

Long and narrow, the hawksbill turtle's head is perfectly designed to forage for sponges in the holes and cracks of coral reefs.

Senses at Work

Sea turtles use a variety of senses to help them find food. The most important sense is probably smell, which is highly developed in all sea turtles. To smell, a sea turtle pulls water into its nostrils. Special receptors pick up scent information and pass it to the turtle's brain. The sea turtle then pushes the water out through its mouth. By using its sense of smell, a sea turtle can find food even when conditions are dark or cloudy.

Sight is a sea turtle's next most important sense. Sea turtles have excellent vision underwater. If conditions are clear, a sea turtle has no trouble spotting potential meals in the water or on the ocean floor. Sea

Sea turtles like this green sea turtle have a highly developed sense of smell and excellent underwater vision and hearing.

turtles cannot see nearly as well when they are out of the water. But since males never leave the ocean, and females leave only to lay eggs, this is not a handicap when it comes to finding food.

Hearing is another sense that sea turtles use when hunting. Although sea turtles do not have external ears, they do have eardrums, and bones inside their heads easily pick up sound vibrations. By listening to the noises around them, sea turtles can detect and pinpoint likely sources of food.

Time to Eat

Once a sea turtle has found food, it gets ready to eat. The sea turtle swims toward the food by flapping its powerful front flippers like wings. It uses its flat back flippers and tail to steer as it moves through the water. Before long the sea turtle is in position to grab its intended meal.

Spotting a tasty sea anemone, a sea turtle reaches out to clamp its strong jaws around its prey.

For green and black sea turtles, the eating process is simple. These plant eaters just close their jaws around tasty sea grasses and pull them loose. Other sea turtles must work a little harder to catch their living, moving meals. But because sea turtles move much more quickly than most of their prey, there is not usually much chasing to do. A sea turtle simply opens its bony beak and clamps its jaws closed on its prey. Some species can also use their jaws to pry stuck shellfish off the ocean floor or pull buried food into the open before biting down. Once the sea turtle has a firm grip on its prey, it may chomp a few times before swallowing, or it may gobble its meal whole.

Of all sea turtle species, the leatherback probably has to work hardest to keep itself fed. A leatherback can eat its own weight in jellyfish each day. This is necessary because jellyfish are made mostly of water and therefore are not very nutritious. Other sea turtles that eat higher-calorie food probably eat much less than leatherbacks do. Still, all sea turtles put a lot of energy into the search for food. Eating keeps a sea turtle strong and healthy, enabling it to survive in the harsh ocean world.

chapter 24

Sea Turtles in Danger

S ea turtles face many threats during their lifetimes. Even before hatching, these animals are in danger from egg-eating predators such as raccoons, foxes, and lizards. Humans may also dig up sea turtle eggs and sell them as food. After hatching, sea turtles face danger from both humans and other animals.

Today, all species of sea turtles are endangered (facing a high risk of extinction) or threatened (likely to become endangered in the near future). A combination of natural and human factors has caused this situation.

A Dangerous Time

All sea turtles are in the greatest danger immediately after hatching. This is the period when small turtles

A pink ghost crab on a South African beach preys on a sea turtle hatchling.

must travel from their nest to the sea. Soft and help-less, the newly hatched turtles are easy prey for hungry animals such as sea birds, crabs, dogs, and raccoons. These predators and others kill up to 90 percent of the babies before they can reach the water's edge.

In modern times, lights from human developments have made the situation worse. Sea turtle hatchlings instinctively head toward light areas, so they may go the wrong way if they see artificial lights. Lost and wandering far from the water, the little turtles are more likely to be found and eaten by predators. Sometimes they even stray onto lighted roadways, where they are struck and killed by passing cars.

Despite these dangers, many sea turtle hatchlings manage to reach the ocean. But these turtles are far from safe. A young sea turtle is likely to be eaten by fish, sea birds, or other predators. It is not until a baby turtle swims far out to sea and hides itself in a mat of seaweed that it is fairly safe and able to start to grow. Very few sea turtles, however, reach this point. Scientists estimate that only one out of every thousand sea turtles survives to adulthood.

Adults as Prey

The lucky sea turtles that do reach adulthood are not easy prey. Adult sea turtles are big compared to most other ocean animals, which makes them difficult to catch and kill. They are also protected by their thick,

The coloration on this hawksbill turtle's shell helps it blend in with the coral to protect it from predators.

hard shells. Between their size and their shells, sea turtles are not very appealing to most predators.

Some species of sea turtles keep themselves even safer with coloring that hides them from predators. Hawksbills and green sea turtles, for example, have dark upper surfaces and light lower surfaces. This type of coloration, called **countershading**, helps a sea turtle to blend into its surroundings. Seen from above, a countershaded turtle disappears against the dark ocean floor. Seen from below, it fades against the brightly lit sea surface.

Despite the sea turtle's many defenses, some creatures do attack these animals. Some large sharks, especially tiger sharks, are known to eat sea turtles. Killer whales may also eat sea turtles. And in South America, jaguars sometimes eat sea turtles that have left the ocean to lay eggs.

In some parts of the world, humans also hunt sea turtles. Green sea turtles are popular in some areas because their fat can be used to make a gourmet soup. Hawksbill turtles are hunted for their beautiful shells, and olive ridleys are killed for their skin, which can be made into a fine leather.

Accidental Harm

Although people do kill some sea turtles on purpose, they kill many more by accident. The fishing industry in particular is a threat to sea turtles. Many sea turtles lose their lives after they get caught in fishermen's nets. Struggling to free themselves, these creatures run out

A man holds up a large adult sea turtle he caught while diving off the coast of Belize.

of air and die within minutes. Other sea turtles become entangled in abandoned fishing gear, such as torn nets and free-floating fishing line. These turtles die if they cannot work their way loose.

Human garbage poses another danger to sea turtles. Turtles eat all sorts of trash, especially see-through plastics, which look like tasty jellyfish. These materials quickly clog a sea turtle's **digestive system** and eventually kill the animal. Sea turtles have also died after poking their heads through the holes in plastic six-pack rings. Over time, as the sea turtle grows, the plastic becomes tighter and tighter around its neck.

Many sea turtles like this young hawksbill lose their lives each year after getting tangled in fishermen's nets.

After a while, the ring is so tight that the sea turtle has trouble eating and breathing. The turtle will die if the ring is not removed.

Another way humans affect sea turtle populations is by preventing females from laying eggs. Some turtles that see unfamiliar lights, buildings, or people on nesting beaches decide not to come ashore. Others leave the ocean but then return when they get too nervous. Called a **false crawl**, this situation means that hundreds of fertilized eggs will never be laid, for once a female gives up and goes back into the sea, she will not come back to finish the job.

Protecting Sea Turtles

Sea turtle protection is a major concern in traditional nesting areas. Many beachside communities, for example, have laws that require residents to dim their lights during nesting times. This encourages sea turtles to nest normally. Once nests have been made, they are surrounded by barriers and signs that warn people to stay away.

Nesting grounds around the world are also being turned into parks or nature reserves. One example is the Archie Carr National Wildlife Refuge along Florida's east coast. An important nesting area for green sea turtles and loggerheads, this refuge plays an important role in keeping populations healthy. Countries including Nicaragua and Costa Rica have also established sea turtle reserves.

Protecting nesting areas is not the only way to keep sea turtles safe. Many countries have passed laws that are designed to protect adult sea turtles, too. In

After being nursed for nine months in a sea turtle hospital in North Carolina, this loggerhead turtle is being returned to the wild.

Turtle Excluder Device (TED)

more than 160 countries, for example, sea turtles are covered by the Convention on International Trade in Endangered Species (CITES). Member nations have agreed to ban the import and export of sea turtles and their products. By removing the market for sea turtles, this ban discourages illegal hunting.

Steps are also being taken to keep sea turtles from getting caught in fishing nets. In the southeastern United States, turtle excluder devices (TEDs) must be built into all shrimp nets. TEDs let shrimp enter a net but allow sea turtles to escape. These devices are very effective, releasing an estimated 97 percent of all sea turtles that accidentally enter shrimp nets. TEDs have been so suc-

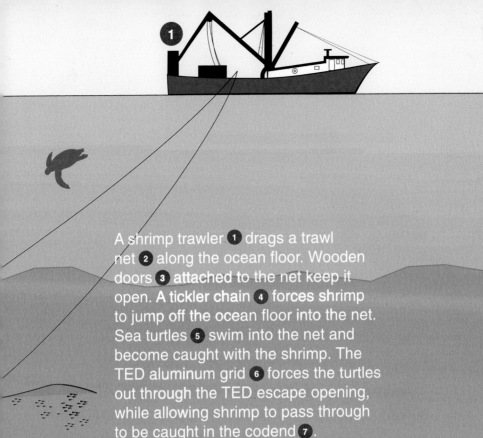

A shrimp trawler ❶ drags a trawl net ❷ along the ocean floor. Wooden doors ❸ attached to the net keep it open. A tickler chain ❹ forces shrimp to jump off the ocean floor into the net. Sea turtles ❺ swim into the net and become caught with the shrimp. The TED aluminum grid ❻ forces the turtles out through the TED escape opening, while allowing shrimp to pass through to be caught in the codend ❼.

cessful in the United States, in fact, that the U.S. National Marine Fisheries Service is working with other countries to set up TED programs. Today about 40 countries require shrimp fishermen to use these devices.

TEDs, sea turtle reserves, and other conservation measures are very important to the long-term health of sea turtle populations. Humans are the greatest threat to sea turtles, so it is only fair that they should take an active role in protecting them. The fossil record shows that sea turtles have been on the earth for more than 200 million years. With a little care and attention, these fascinating creatures will be around for many millions of years yet to come.

Glossary

arribadas: Mass nestings of Kemp's ridleys and olive ridleys.

carapace: The upper side of the sea turtle's shell.

countershading: Coloration that is darker on top and lighter on the bottom.

Cryptodira: The scientific suborder to which all sea turtles belong.

digestive system: An animal's system that breaks down food.

embryos: Developing sea turtles before they hatch.

false crawl: When a female sea turtle returns to the sea before completing the nesting process.

hibernate: To spend the winter in a resting state.

keratin: A hard protein from which sea turtles' scutes are made.

lost year: In sea turtles' lives, the period between hatching and young adulthood.

plastron: The lower side of the sea turtle's shell.

scutes: Hard scales that cover the sea turtle's carapace.

swimming frenzy: One to two days of continuous swimming after sea turtle hatchlings enter the water for the first time.

For Further Exploration

Books

Kathryn Lasky, *Interrupted Journey: Saving Endangered Sea Turtles*. Cambridge, MA: Candlewick Press, 2001. The true story of a team of veterinarians, marine biologists, and volunteers who save a sick Kemp's ridley sea turtle.

Sara Swan Miller, *Turtles: Life in a Shell*. New York: Franklin Watts, 1999. Includes descriptions of fifteen turtle species and recommendations for finding, identifying, and observing them.

Liz Palika, *Turtles & Tortoises for Dummies*. New York: Hungry Minds, 2001. All the information anyone needs to raise a healthy turtle.

Sandra Robbins, *How the Turtle Got Its Shell: An African Tale*. Roslyn, NY: Berrent Publications, 1990. Based on a traditional African tale, this book tells how turtle Akykiegie tricks the leopard Osebo, wins the approval of the Sky God Nyame, and earns his hard shell.

Web Sites

Caribbean Conservation Corporation, Sea Turtle Migration-Tracking Education Program (www.ccc. turtle.org/sat1.htm). This site uses satellite data to track real sea turtles around the Caribbean islands. Includes current maps of the turtles' locations.

Turtle Trax, Sea Turtles for Kids (www.turtles. org/kids.htm). Includes lots of links to sea turtle stories, games, webcams, and more.

Index